"Who knew we were embarrassing him so much?"

—**Etta and Ralph DiGiorgia**, parents, Teaneck, NJ

"Thanks to this book, I can bring my friends home without first sending my parents to a movie."

—**Blake DiGiorgia**, teenager, Teaneck, NJ

The time to stop embarrassing your kids is right now! You can begin by following Rule #1, which is: DON'T stand in the middle of a bookstore, reading this book and laughing to yourself! Go to the counter, buy it, and start giving your kids the break they deserve!

HOW NOT TO EMBARRASS YOUR KIDS

250 Don'ts for Parents of Teens

ZACK ELIAS & TRAVIS GOLDMAN

WARNER BOOKS

A Time Warner Company

Copyright © 1999 by Zack Elias and Travis Goldman

All rights reserved.

Warner Books, Inc., 1271 Avenue of the Americas, New York, NY 10020

Visit our Web site at warnerbooks.com

 A Time Warner Company

Printed in the United States of America

First Printing: May 1999

10 9 8 7 6 5 4 3

Library of Congress Cataloging-in-Publication Data
Elias, Zack.
How not to embarrass your kids : 250 don'ts for parents of teens / Zack Elias & Travis Goldman.
p. cm.
ISBN 0-446-67503-2
1. Embarrassment in adolescence. 2. Parent and teenager.
I. Goldman, Travis. II. Title.
BF724. 3.E45E55 1999
649.125—dc21   98-48305
CIP

Cover and text design by Bernadette Evangelist
Cover and text illustrations by Jared D. Lee

Dedication

To Oreo, Sandy, Snowflake, and Bunga
In memory of Razzle and Hercules

Acknowledgments

We'd like to thank the following people who helped to make this project possible: our parents and our sisters. Also, Bernadette Evangelist, Karla Doughtery, Stephanie Tade, John Aherne, Melanie Braggard, Ben Pearce, Jenna Mayer, Pamela, Omi, Grandpa Joe, Nana, Grandpa Saul, Grandma Anita, Grandpa Jackie, Mel Brooks, Bill Buckner, and Scott Norwood.

Contents

Introduction

How many times have we turned to each other and said, "You won't believe what my mom was wearing this morning," or "I nearly died of embarrassment last night when I was with my dad!" How many times have we dreaded being seen with our parents for fear of being humiliated, only to have that fear fulfilled? How many times have we tried to explain to our parents that what they do and wear and eat, and their general presence, is embarrassing for *us*, their teenaged children? And yet they continue to embarrass us each and every day.

During the particularly gruelling summer of '97 when we were both sixteen, we realized that not only do our parents not humiliate us intentionally, but also they are actually oblivious to our steady discomfort. We then realized that maybe we, living, breathing, mortified teens, could help our parents to ease our suffering. We decided to provide them (and other parents coping with the same struggle) with a comprehensive list of DON'Ts—250 to be exact—so they could avoid destroying their teen children on a day-to-day basis.

We hope that the suggestions in this book will lessen some of the trauma of having parents during one's teenage years. We understand that no one can totally eradicate this steady embarrassment. These suggestions have worked for us and our friends, and we hope they will also work for you.

I. Private & Personal Matters

When we were little and you explained how Mommy and Daddy needed privacy, you always told us that "everyone needs privacy." Of course, being little we didn't need or want any, so it was a pretty safe explanation. Now when we tell you that something is private, you act like it's such a big deal and tend to mock us for wanting privacy. Aren't we part of "everyone"? We want privacy and we need privacy, and the best way for you to deal is by listening when we say:

1. Don't ask.

2. DON'T ASK.

3. Don't EVER come into our bedroom.

4. Don't pretend to need a pen and paper and go looking through our backpack.

5. Don't ask who we sat with at lunch.

6. Don't make a whole big thing when you ask us what we did at school all day and we answer "nothing." For example, don't ever say "Obviously you did something or you wouldn't have been at school for six hours" or "OK, so you just sat and looked at the wall all day?"

7. Don't ask if we got a test back.

8. Don't ask details about anything—because either we don't remember or we don't care.

9. Don't make an issue of anything unless it is totally life threatening like crack or heroin (finding a pack of cigarettes is not totally life threatening).

10. Don't pretend to like our music. And if you really do like our music, don't tell anyone.

11. Don't ever say that all our music sounds the same.

12. Don't pretend to like the things we like (MTV, *Beavis and Butthead*, *South Park*, etc.).

13. Don't reminisce about your hippie days.

14. Don't ask us where we are going when we go out. If we want you to know we'll tell you on our own.

15. Don't always remind us not to do drugs or drink whenever we go out.

16. Don't ask any questions after a party.

17. Don't make us read all the newspaper and magazine articles about problem teens.

18. Don't fix our clothes, straighten our tie or tuck in our shirt, in public.

19. Don't lick your finger to wipe *schmootz* off our face.

20. Don't ever ask us if we made a BM during the day.

21. Don't ever blame the pet or anyone else (you know what we're talking about).

22. Don't name us something stupid (especially something you think is cute or trendy).

II. When We Are with Our Friends

Just because you are really happy when (if) we come in and sit around with you when your friends are visiting, do not assume that the reverse is true. When we have friends over, please try to remember that they are visiting us. They haven't come over to sit around awkwardly and be polite to anyone's parents. And they haven't come over to see more of you than just a quick "hi." So, when our friends are hanging at our house, please, please:

1. **Don't** wear weird sandals, especially the floppy ones, because no one visiting wants to hear you flapping around.

2. **Don't** walk around in a bathrobe or your underwear.

3. **Don't** wear perfume in the house when our friends are

over because then the whole place reeks.

4. Don't baby us or our friends.

5. Don't offer our friends money. It makes them feel awkward because you are treating them like children.

6. Don't give us money in front of our friends. Try to give it to us before anyone else is around. And don't always ask if we have enough money; we'll always ask if we need more.

7. Don't make jokes unless you are absolutely sure they are funny.

8. Don't come near one of our parties.

9. Don't sit down to join us during a video.

10. Don't ask a lot of questions about friends' families.

11. Don't call us by your pet nicknames in front of our friends.

12. Don't take an interest in our friends; they have no interest in you.

13. Don't show our friends our baby pictures/home videos or tell them cute things we did when we were little.

14. Don't start to cry when you give a speech (such as at our bas/bar mitzvah or first communion).

15. Don't ask our friends for their opinion on current events.

16. Don't kiss our friends.

17. Don't laugh at your own jokes.

18. Don't tell us when to go to sleep when a friend is sleeping over.

19. Don't say kootchy-kootchy-koo to the family pet if a friend is over.

20. Don't ask us to change the cat's litter in front of a friend. Don't do it yourself either.

21. Don't ask us to walk the dog when we are with a friend.

III. Fashion

Let's be honest here for just a moment. Did Grandma and Grandpa like what you wore when you were in high school? Did they ever come close to "getting it" about your taste in clothes? No, of course not. So, we don't expect you to be any different than they were—we don't expect you to like our clothes or understand them. Actually, if you can ever understand and try to remember the following thoughts, we've come close to bridging the generation-fashion gap:

1. Don't buy us anything to wear that is not dark and muddy colored.

2. Don't ever buy us anything that has flowers on it. Flowered clothes are only acceptable in Hawaii.

3. Don't even buy clothes for us; just give us the money and we'll buy our own.

4. Don't point to another kid whose shirt is

tucked in and say how nice he/she looks.

5. Don't tell us that everyone always takes his/her hat off when they come inside.

6. Don't ask why we don't want to wear something, especially if we wore it last year or last month.

7. **Don't** wear our clothes.

8. **Don't** wear bell bottoms.

9. **Don't** wear bright-colored flowered shirts (especially Dads).

10. **Don't** wear safari hats, especially in the city.

11. **Don't** wear tight pants.

12. In fact, **don't** wear tight anything.

13. **Don't** wear pants that stop above the ankle.

14. **Don't** wear shirts that show cleavage or chest hair.

15. **Don't** even try to explain why you need so

many different pairs of shoes.

16. **Don't** ever wear your hair in a beehive, or any style that is high or wide.

17. **Don't** let your nose or ear hair grow so it's noticeable . . . keep it trimmed.

18. **Don't** wear anything from the previous decade, unless you are going to a costume party.

19. **Don't** wear sports or team jerseys.

20. **Don't** wear anything that tries to make you look younger because you won't fool anyone.

21. **Don't** wear anything leather . . . especially a skirt, pants, a dress, or a vest.

22. Don't wear so much jewelry that you jingle when you move your arms.

23. Don't pretend that you aren't going gray by dyeing your hair.

24. Don't comb your hair to hide the bald spot— it's obvious what you're hiding even without the wind.

25. Don't have more than ten keys on your key chain; you're not a dungeon master.

IV. Shopping

Don't offer to take us shopping after you've had a really bad day at work or on the second day after you've quit smoking. We, on the other hand, would prefer not to shop during playoff games or on a day when we have lots of zits or bad hair. Shopping together will never be an activity that bridges or lessens the generation gap, but it need not be a disaster if you can try to remember these few suggestions:

1. Don't ask the salesperson for something "cool."

2. Don't pull everything off the rack to show your kid and ask "Do you like this?"

3. Don't say how expensive the clothes are in front of the salesperson.

4. Don't ever come into the dressing room.

5. Don't ask us to come out of the dressing room so you can see how something fits or looks. If we want your opinion, we'll come out on our own.

6. Don't comment on the quality of the clothes in front of the salesperson.

7. Don't point to what another kid is trying on and say "Doesn't that look nice—do you want to try it on?"

8. Don't tell the salesperson your life story or your kid's life story.

9. Don't call out our name real loud in the store; if we get separated, look for us silently.

10. Don't go crazy at the check-out line if it doesn't move quickly.

11. Don't suggest we buy two of something if we like it.

12. Don't buy clothes for us if we are not there.

13. Don't buy something just because it's on sale.

14. Don't say that you will wait to buy something when it goes on sale; buy it when your kid wants it.

15. Don't ask out loud if our underwear is too small yet. In fact, don't ask at all.

16. Don't mention the crotch or bosom of anything we try on.

17. Don't talk to anyone who your kid knows from school.

18. Don't ask another kid where they got what they're wearing.

V. Watching TV

How many times have you criticized how much we watch TV and what shows we prefer? Maybe you need to accept that, in just the way you don't consider Coke and Doritos to be the basic staples of a healthy diet, you really don't understand our basic TV needs. Not everything can be explained by Dr. Freud and Dr. Spock (not the Vulcan). If you can accept the following rules, and let us watch TV in peace, then harmony will permeate the house (as long as we control the remote):

1. **Don't** ever tell us TV rots our brain.

2. **Don't** ever tell us we'll get a "TV head" from watching too much.

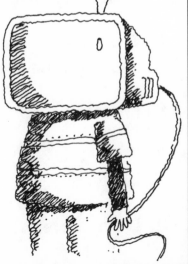

3. **Don't** ever say "couch potato"; at least be creative and say "spud" or "'tator."

4. **Don't** ever tell us we are

watching too much TV—we will know when we've watched too much.

5. Don't ever comment on the quality of our shows.

6. Don't object to TV during meals by saying it's more fun to chat with the family. TV is always better than family conversations.

7. Don't ever come in in the middle of a show and ask a lot of questions about what's gone on.

8. Don't say something we laugh at is not funny.

9. Don't take offense at anything derogatory we laugh at.

10. Don't ever say how fake professional wrestling

is while we we're watching and enjoying it.

11. Don't ever watch TV with us uninvited.

12. Don't ever dominate the remote.

13. Don't ever sit in our spot while watching TV with us. In fact, don't sit in our spot even when we are not around. (You may alter the butt groove that took us years to forge.)

14. Don't start to read and crinkle the newspaper while you are watching TV with us.

15. Don't ever say when we are using the remote "You're going too fast; I can't see what's on."

16. Don't watch the Discovery Channel, the Learning Channel, the History Channel, or PBS.

17. Don't use your index finger to work the remote—always use your thumb.

18. Don't get mad if we need to change the channel to get the score.

19. Don't make a comment if what we are watching contains violence or nudity.

20. Don't change the channel if something scary is

about to happen. Just suck it up.

21. Don't try to start a conversation with us while we are watching a sporting event.

22. Don't comment on how boring a football/baseball/basketball/hockey game is. It's not boring to us.

23. Don't comment on how boring *any* sporting event is unless it's soccer, women's golf, or NASCAR.

VI. At the Movies

Going to the movies with you is one of those rare activities where our embarrassment can be minimal. After all, most theaters are large (supporting the "you-can't-notice-everyone-in-the-crowd" theory) and dark (an obvious safety factor). But because we must enter, sit, and exit together, there can still be some opportunities for us to prefer execution. This can be eliminated if you will just follow these simple guidelines:

1. Don't wear a big hat or big hair.

2. Don't describe the movie by who is in it or where it takes place when buying a ticket—always use the name of the movie.

3. Don't see any movie if one of the main stars is from the TV show *Friends*.

4. Don't ever turn down the supercombo.

5. Don't buy the hot dogs, which have been sitting there since before the Chicago Cubs won the World Series.

6. Don't ever buy Jujubees or Jujyfruits.

7. Don't make a big deal out of picking a seat. Just pick one and sit down.

8. Don't sit in the make-out seats.

9. Don't sit in the first or last row.

10. Don't yell out the answers to the pre-movie trivia quiz show.

11. Don't sing along with the pre-movie music.

12. Don't ever comment on the previews. Just sit there and watch.

13. Don't try to make a bootleg video.

14. Don't get up more than once during the movie.

15. Don't laugh unless everyone else is laughing.

16. Don't sigh out loud if you don't understand something during the movie.

17. Don't talk during the movie unless you are making fun of someone.

18. Don't grab our hands or cover our eyes in tense or scary situations.

19. Don't forget that they are just actors and they aren't really getting killed (except for Brandon Lee).

20. Don't get up to leave when you think the movie is over—wait for the credits to start, in case you are wrong. And once they start rolling, don't wait for all the credits to see who played what—just leave when the first credit comes on.

21. Don't run to the exits when the movie is over—just walk out normally.

22. Don't clap at the end of the movie.

23. Don't expect discussion about the movie after it is over. There needs to be at least a one-week grace period.

24. Don't ever compare the movie to the original version. The original is always better than the sequel (except for *Terminator*).

VII. Driving

Driving around with you doesn't have to be embarrassing or awkward. It will probably be both, but at least it doesn't have to be totally humiliating. Until we are of legal age, we need you to drive us around—to hang out with friends, to go to the movies, or to take us to ball games. Sitting in the car with you doesn't have to be one of the worst things we can imagine, especially if you remember all of the following:

1. Don't put the convertible top down when driving your teen around no matter how warm and sunny it is. If it's that hot, just turn on the a/c.

2. Don't buy a bright-colored sports car just to look younger.

3. At toll booths, **don't**:

- talk with the toll booth person: don't ask how they are, don't sympathize with how hot they must be

- continue to sing along out loud to the radio

- use the rearview mirror to put on lipstick or pick your teeth

- comment on how expensive the toll is (never say "That's highway robbery")

4. Don't let your hair fly sideways out the windows.

5. Don't ever take the scenic route; always stick to the highway.

6. Don't call being lost "an adventure."

7. Don't ask for directions.

8. Don't ride around and around the parking lot looking for the perfect space; just park in the first empty spot.

9. Don't try for the "perfect pump" when filling the car with gas; JUST DO IT!

10. Don't use the steering wheel as a drum or the dashboard as a keyboard.

11. Don't sing out loud to the golden oldies.

12. Don't make your kid nervous while teaching him/her how to drive.

VIII. Family Vacations

"**F**amily vacations are fun." "Travel is sooo broadening." "You can learn more on a weeklong family vacation than doing almost anything else during that time." "Family vacations are a terrific bonding experience." How many speeches have we heard beginning with statements like these? Actually, some family vacations can be fun and even "stimulating" and "informative," but only if you:

1. Don't try to speak more than one word in any foreign language when visiting that country. For example, when in Spain do not ask "*dónde está* the little girl's room?"

2. Don't take on the local customs of the country you are visiting. For example, when in Paris, don't go around kissing everyone on both cheeks, and don't wear a beret.

3. Don't look like an obvious tourist: no short shorts with high tube socks; no glasses with sunglass clip-ons; no dorky hats just resting atop your head; no fanny packs; no asking directions and walking around with a map opened up; no wearing brand-new T-shirts from the place you are visiting.

4. Don't buy a fancy new camera with a lens and a tripod for a weeklong trip.

5. Don't look all night for the perfect restaurant: They are all unknown; so just pick one.

6. Don't wear any hats with feathers in them. You are not a tribal leader.

7. Don't become the tour guide for the family.

8. Don't tell us that there will be kids our age "there"; NEVER try to introduce us to any of them.

9. Don't be a gringo.

IX. Eating in Restaurants

When we are hungry you only need to feed us. It's food we crave, not a "dining experience." An Extra Value Meal will always be fine. Eating with you in a restaurant needn't be more stressful than eating with you at home, nor does it have to be unendurably long and boring, but you'll have to follow these basic rules:

1. Don't order anything that is expensive if someone else is paying.

2. Don't order anything on the menu just because it is written in another language. Know what you are ordering and be able to pronounce it correctly.

3. Don't send food back more than once.

4. Don't snap your fingers to get the waiter's attention or yell out "boy" or "miss."

5. Don't complain about the service while your teens are still sitting at the table.

6. Don't laugh really loudly.

7. Don't talk to people you don't know who are sitting at the next or nearby table.

8. Don't tell your life story to the waiter.

9. Don't clean your ears or your teeth with the straw from your drink.

10. Don't tell the waiter how good the food is. He doesn't care and he won't bother to relay the message to the chef.

11. Don't have a major discussion about who will pay the bill.

X. At the Beach

Going to the beach can be OK (if you like hot sand, freezing water, and gritty snacks). For some it can be relaxing to just lie back and chill listening to the sounds of the surf (and a Discman). But the beach will never be relaxing or fun if you forget that any of the following are total "day ruiners":

1. Don't wear a bikini or thong bathing suit.

2. Don't wear a white bathing suit, because it gets see-through when wet.

3. Don't change into your bathing suit on the beach.

4. Don't use an umbrella that has fish or other cute designs; if you

must use an umbrella, use only solids or stripes.

5. Don't wade in only up to your ankles (and then sprinkle a little water on your shoulders); either stay on the beach or dive in.

6. Don't snorkle, and if you do, don't put on the mask or flippers until you are completely in the water.

7. Don't bring a huge radio, or a small radio that plays loudly.

8. Don't bring a beach ball. No one wants to see a group of middle-aged people with guts hanging over playing catch.

9. Don't try to get us excited to build a sand castle; face it, mud castles with moats are not that exciting.

10. Don't use any sunblock higher than 15, because everyone knows it is all the same after that.

11. Don't try to put suntan lotion on our face or ears; wait until we figure out that these parts burn.

12. Don't pick up other people's garbage.

13. Don't continue to remind us that we need to wait one hour to swim after lunch; let us figure it out when we get cramps.

XI. Family Recreational Activities

Family sports are tolerable if limited to activities in which we all keep moving, since the likelihood of our seeing (or being seen) by anyone we know is diminished by our perpetual motion. Croquet, catch-Frisbee, and horseshoes, however, are less than desirable. But in order for us not to spend the entire time dreading some outdoor blunder that will make us wish we were orphans, please read these rules and take them to heart:

1. Don't try to do any tricks.

2. Don't put any stickers or fruity laces on your Rollerblades.

3. Don't put an electronic meter on your bike that tells you your heart rate, your caloric burn, your breathing rate, your speed, your altitude, your distance, the lunar calendar, or the tempera-ture on Saturn. You'll look like a doofus since you are only riding half a mile to pick up milk and are not in a triathlon.

4. Don't try to show off (for example, when playing football, don't yell "Go for it!").

5. Don't try to learn our sports (i.e., skateboarding, Rollerblading, etc.) because if you do, worlds will collide.

6. Don't snowboard.

7. Don't ever wear white when skiing.

8. Don't wear anything bright or neon-colored, even at night—this isn't the '80s.

9. Don't buy any funky-shaped ski hats—just a plain old headband will do.

10. Don't use any equipment that singles you out:
like using sled dogs when everyone else is skiing
or snowboarding.

11. Don't stop for us if we fall; just keep going and
as you pass say "Meet you at the bottom."

12. Don't wave or call
our name from the
chairlift.

13. Don't talk to the ski
instructor about our
progress.

14. Don't ever ask
another kid to teach
us something.

15. Don't buy the most expensive gear and outfits when just beginning a new sport.

16. Don't wear short tennis outfits.

17. Don't try to give your kid lessons while you are playing tennis, baseball, etc., together.

18. Don't ask a random instructor who is teaching a class or someone else's kid to help your kid.

XII. Ball Games & Sporting Events

It can sometimes be a bit awkward, but we really don't mind going with you to a football or a basketball game. Well, it's OK as long as you don't totally mortify us. If you don't think you'll be able to abide by the following rules, it's far better to stay home—even at the risk of missing a great game. Nothing is worth public humiliation because you didn't understand the following:

1. **Don't** bring a newspaper or magazine (or worse, a book) from home. Why waste your money on a ticket if you're not going to watch the game?

2. **Don't** bring your own food or beverages.

3. **Don't** wave "creative" signs to get on TV. It's OK if we go to the game together but there is no need for you to try to make a public spectacle of yourself.

4. Don't make an ass of yourself if you do get on TV.

5. Don't cheer unless everyone else is also cheering.

6. Don't scream anything to your favorite player because they can't hear you anyway.

7. Don't yell out anything witty unless you are sure it is really witty.

8. Don't put your coat and briefcase

or shopping bags on the seats next to you, because it will be really awkward and we'll feel like jerks when someone comes to sit there.

9. Don't move closer to the front unless you are positive no one is coming back to claim those seats, because you'll feel incredibly stupid when the usher comes asking if those seats are yours.

10. Don't make conversation with the people sitting near you; don't try to show off your sports knowledge.

11. Don't tell us how great sports were back when you were young. We don't care.

XIII. Extracurricular Sports & Activities

I t is not necessary for you to come to any weekend sports practices, but we do insist that you come to watch all of our games, recitals, performances, etc. We want you to stand inconspicuously on the side and watch and be proud. And, have fun. But if fun means you need to do any of the following, forget the fun and just watch and be proud (you can have fun someplace else):

1. Don't cheer.

2. Don't cheer, but if you have to cheer, cheer for everyone, not just your kid.

3. Don't run on to the field or have sideline hysterics if your kid gets hurt or messes up.

4. Don't ever call time out.

5. Don't argue with the ref. In fact, don't even talk to the ref.

6. Don't discuss your kid's progress with the coach. In fact, don't even talk to the coach.

7. Don't bring a team snack of quartered oranges and water; just bring doughnuts and Gatorade.

8. Don't ever volunteer to coach a Little League team, but if you absolutely have to coach, no nepotism.

9. Don't try to cheer up your kid if he/she has somehow screwed up; you can't make him/her feel better.

10. Don't ever say "It's not who wins, it's how you play the game," because every kid knows that "winning is everything."

XIV. Parents' Day at School & Other School Rules

Your boss has never invited us to spend a day at your office and we prefer that our schools discontinue inviting you to our classrooms. Parents' Day at school is torture for us, and for you it's like walking through a Cambodian minefield: every step (or word or gesture) could produce humiliation and disaster. Even if you stick to all of the following rules, parents in school are about as welcome as Nicorette in a French café.

1. Don't walk in during the middle of the class and wave at your child. He/she will know you've arrived even without the wave.

2. Don't volunteer for "career day" if you have a boring job.

3. Don't start an argument with the teacher.

4. Don't correct the

teacher if he/she makes a mistake.

5. Don't raise your hand to answer a question; in fact, don't answer anything.

6. Don't try to sympathize with any parents who you do not know.

7. Don't be friendly with parents unless the kids are friends.

8. Don't talk to the teacher after class.

9. Don't kiss, hug, or show any

affection to your child anywhere on school grounds.

10. **Don't** admit to being lost as you go from class to class; always pretend to know where you are going.

11. **Don't** let your cell phone or beeper go off during a class. And worse, don't answer it and try to whisper a conversation.

12. **Don't** make your teen go to school if he/she doesn't feel well.

13. **Don't** ever show up at school unannounced.

14. **Don't** run into the middle of a class to bring something we forgot at home no matter how important it is.

XV. Homework

Is there an eleventh commandment just for parents stating that "they shalt always nag-even-to-the-point-of-torture" their teens about homework? You might have to learn to trust us a little more, especially when we say we have finished all of our homework or that we weren't assigned any. You need to stay calm, try and relax, and not let homework become an all-night, every-night battle zone. This certainly won't be easy, but it's not impossible if you try to adhere to the following:

1. **Don't** ever help us unless we ask you to.

2. **Don't** make it a long painful ordeal when we ask for math help. Don't walk us through *all* the steps.

3. **Don't** keep explaining once we've started to cry.

4. **Don't** tell us how many A's you got or

how many hours a night you did your homework.

5. Don't nag us more than twice an evening about how much homework we have.

6. Don't make up homework for us to do.

7. Don't ever make us do homework that is not due the next day.

8. Don't make us study two weeks in advance for a minor quiz.

9. Don't quiz us repeatedly and don't go nuts when we miss an accent mark.

10. Don't tell us how easy a test is going to be, because if we fail, we'll feel like total losers.

11. Don't ever go through our essays with your glasses on and a red pencil in hand.

12. Don't ever say, while editing our papers, "What are you doing here?" or "This makes no sense!"

13. Don't criticize before you finish reading the paragraph.

14. Don't make us rewrite an essay if we got a bad grade.

15. Don't tell us we have to study in our room at our desk; where we put ourselves is where we want to study.

16. Don't say we studied for fifteen minutes if we say it was for an hour.

17. Don't tell us we didn't study enough—we know how much to study because we know how big the test is.

18. Don't always disagree when we question the point or use of calculus or physics or chemistry or ethics or school in general.

19. Don't get mad at us while you are editing or retyping our paper and we are busy playing with our pet or chatting on the phone.